RIGHT AS RAIN

Right as Rain

Luellen Fletcher

Right as Rain

Library of Congress Control Number:		2021906104
ISBN:	Hardcover	978-1-6641-6499-4
	Softcover	978-1-6641-6498-7
	eBook	978-1-6641-6497-0

Print information available on the last page.

Rev. date: 04/09/2021

To order additional copies of this book, contact:
Xlibris
844-714-8691
www.Xlibris.com
Orders@Xlibris.com
813656

for Maya and Bob

Nothing in the world is permanent, and we're foolish when we ask anything to last, but surely, we're still more foolish not to take delight in it while we have it.

– W. Somerset Maugham, *The Razor's Edge*

Acknowledgements

Special thanks to Marjory Werner, Elizabeth Snell, Susan Staggs, Leslie Elliott, Mariska Bogle, Marnie Miller and Susan Williams, Penn and Pencil Club, my Philadelphia Tribune colleagues, Robert Woods Bogle and family.

In Memoriam: Karen Murphy, David Snell, Marie Kanalas Bogle, Fred and Lila Fletcher.

Leaving Edinburgh on the Evening Train
   1st Prize Bell Jar Poetry Contest, *Ampersand Magazine* (spring 1979)

Confession
   Muse Letter (spring 1989)

Weightless
   Wisconsin Review (spring 1991)

The World Series
   Spitball (spring 1994)

The Robin of the System
   Blue Hour Press (spring 2014)

Indefinitely
   Blue Hour Press (winter 2015)

David and Coltrane at Work
   P&LM Newsletter (spring 2020)

TABLE OF CONTENTS

The Architecture of Music

None of it is easy except for the momentary spark within the eternal song.
— Howe Gelb, *Piano Influences*

As God would have it, there was a plain
Bank of nature over scored

Where one note led
The other down a pike-invested trail

To understand, philistines frothed,
Fireflies went blind,

But it was no miracle—just mathematics
Of a language holding forth—

Each sum winding down the tongue-tied zero
Each altitude higher than the one before

I forced you into the invisible choir
I wanted you to know something

To hear a singing way beyond you
Forcing water down the lonely grip

To find a future there
Understanding rain

Virtual Walk

My daughter and I planned a virtual walk,
she in her city, I in mine.
As most plans are, ours was flawed.

She phoned early; I was still miles from the forest.
It's ok, she said, *let's talk now as I walk home.*
I heard the metro bus go by,

I heard anchors falling to the streets.
Just city sounds, she said, out of breath, launching
into a funny story. I parked my car,

as she turned the key in her lock, pulled lunch
from her refrigerator. Spurts of laughter, then quiet,
as she thought about what I'd said.

We were together this way for an hour or so,
said our goodbyes, and I set forth
into the cold.

Our favorite filly, eating, as usual, gazes up as I call out,
Hey there, Pretty Girl,
her soft rubbery lips gumming the hay.

A gaucho leads two draft horses toward the stables.
Thunder and Elliott get to eat their lunch inside the barn.
They sleep outside.

Usually, my daughter and I linger near the horses,
waiting for one to eye us,
so we are known.

Today I find a trail behind the field,
follow muddy grooves
where horses carrying paying guests have tread.

A small brown bird, stock-still in her nest,
hides as though I threaten her chicks.
Their speckly screen is safe with me.

Wind comes up behind me, growling rushing air.
I've a winsome idea of this unknown path
that must lead somewhere.

It winds suddenly right, upward
into a grand, thick wood,
far from pastures.

Once hiking with my sisters in the Porcupine Mountains,
as the sun set, they were nervous that we were lost.
Upset with me, Big Sister.

But we weren't lost—I knew—
we were on a trail through Michigan's Upper Peninsula.
North, West, East, South.

Robert Frost's path less travelled
is one way to look at it.
Another is the reward of any path, its surprises.

Around a bend I take into full view a river,
chortling through reeds,
cutting the stones with its being.

A runner passes me, *On your left...*
gives me hope this trail is a wraparound.
But as I near highway buttresses, he swings back into view.

I reach a trailhead map.
In a few miles Hunting Hill, archery grounds and grotto,
so I turn back.

Now I encounter adults, children, dogs…
Don't worry, he's friendly, won't jump.
Gosh, don't I know a friendly dog when I see one?

Giovanni da Verrazzano, Magellan, Da Gama
They had that edge; yes, fearing monsters,
falling off the earth's plane,

but everything they saw was
its first time seen.
I'm thankful to escape the internet.

I'm grateful the river still bristles, fire on ice,
and softens in shadow like a child's whittled toy.
What a bold claim to lay all the difference on the path more or less taken
or not.

I say get lost to be found.
Any view ahead that moves us forward
is enough.

Good Morning Poem

−after a Kalapuya artisan at the Oregon Country Fair

Good morning, Golden Bear.
At six we watch you cross the river,
cleansing your paws in the cold, white water.
Later, when we are busy with our happiness,
you amble across the sky in search of nothing.
We remember, as you sleep in the hills,
your breath now caught inside each leaf,
and we run about in the darkness,
laughing and dancing
as you did.

The Man Wearing Chester Bennington's Shirt

–for Shawn Radtke

In a small bar you could find anywhere
I pulled up for a drink
next to the man wearing
Chester Bennington's shirt.
"Chester's go-to shirt," he said
as we became friendly
in that space between
one shot and three.
"Chester would grab
this moth-eaten jersey,
from ex-girlfriend or wise aunt
to write *less like you*
more like me."
Sleeves too long,
Edges unravelling,
grey collar rimmed thinly.
Faded stars winked
from half-hearted pocket.
The broad back spelled out
"NO SHAME!"

"Feel it—go ahead!"
So downy I touched
for seconds way too long.
"Close to magic," he said.
Whole cloth imagining
I dredged up salt tears
spicy, inside panicking,
to censor the obvious.
He laser-eyed the Jack
"I have cancer.
When I told Chester…"
This man's sudden throatiness—

There went a boiled egg, whole.
"Only way Chester felt safe
was in another skin
of someone loving him.
To compose *Crawling*—
he drove through the middle of his skull
to find its end…"
Mindlessly, I crotch-shopped
silver eagle belt buckle
heavy and knobbed as prison chain.
"He's our Wordsworth—
our Hart Crane…"
Rogue courage cleared my lips.
The man's glossy eyes seemed to register.
"I hear Chester…
Hey Man, you have the meat
in you, the jelly…"

Neither of us was sober, yet
well outside the scope of intoxication.
The clarity of the wooden bar
ornately scavenged snakes and pyre
young men leaning on pool cues
background music all drums—
this moment fantasized most real
myth perpetuated by alcohol, any substance sublime,
that you can walk off a bridge
into water and lift
just your soul
onto wave-crest singing
never waking on shore
just driftwood bumping alongside
to float forever bodiless.
Moonlight will not shock but peel
layers away with gentle fingers
and you, a thumping, permeable insight.

No clear exit now.
The man wearing Chester Bennington's shirt
covering my hand with his
warm as an iron
on low press,
pushing back his stool
Lil darlin' no worries
Chester is here—stabbing his chest—
and here—squashing my hand.
His Chester imploded
We all have a story
A need to be heard
Fans follow me around
I'm no role model
They need to be stronger than I am
Wherever I go please don't
Wear this shirt
Wear this shirt

The man wearing Chester Bennington's shirt
didn't swagger or stumble.
He glided to the door
as a line makes its plane.
My eyes blurred "NO SHAME."
After him, I stepped
into clear moonless space.
Gravel crackled, red lights faded,
night's oaken cask sealed,
port lights rounding a cove
still air, ground animals routing
leaves—I sniffed chimney fire, skunk
and wood beetle.

What do I know?
How do I know it?

Precious privacy between our ears...
shadow of a waving hand,
ashes from buttercups,
we burn we hurt.
I can only begin
where, for me, it began,
next to the man
wearing Chester Bennington's shirt.

Right as Rain

My daughter is usually right
My three key chains should be conjoined
to keep me organized
Countless times she's watched me
dig into my purse for keys and train tickets
invariably dropping a critical scrap of paper on the ground
bending over, bumping into someone behind me
bumbling back up, losing my balance
I embarrass her when she's beside me,
but it also happens when she's not here
her blink of distaste and pity

Am I unable, or unwilling, to challenge symptoms
of unsophisticated lumbering
as she Ubers obliquely to karaoke bars
for Shanghai mojitos in tall wet glasses with ferny mint?
How can I compete with her modern capability?
Or imagine I've had anything to do with her beautiful presence on earth?

Why are you always looking up into the sky like you're lost?

My daughter can't be in my mind and know the patient sacrifice and plotting
routine moments washing her clothes, cooking her vegetables
helping with fractions and dioramas
time I would have spent reconfiguring language in poetry and style
When she was twelve, she said

If you were a real writer there'd be a book on the shelf with your name on it

My daughter is usually right
When I was twelve, I plunked away on a rented piano
as my parents disintegrated upstairs in alcohol-fomented torment

Cold dark dampness
from the outside world I appeared their treasure
Since then, I gravitate toward basements
where no one else will be
I realize today as something of an adult
to mother a child is
squeezing love, a prize in a contest you didn't enter—
wanting your child to feel that way about you
but what she feels is something you don't know
mixture of dependence, insecurity, pride
you're only guessing
a pull in the night, gurgling out of a waking dream

When she speaks to me
my daughter is usually right
but there is much she doesn't say
so, these keys
house keys, work keys, car keys
on three separate chains
two of them ridiculously ugly
except the chain she brought me from the Egyptian museum
I moved house keys onto a Navajo gecko ring—
spirit guide buried too long in a dark bureau—
and from the other removed all interlocks but one
still, I can't seem to put three chains together
and every day I leave one at home and lose another in my bag
My daughter is right
but I persist in my wrongness
to save the self that saved me

I tell my daughter that I'm writing her a poem today
and the first line is
My daughter is always right
I send a photo of the keys
and I can hear her laughing texting back
Lol hahaha I am right!
I can make my daughter laugh
right again, right as rain*

The allusion in this simile is unclear, but it originated in Britain, where rainy weather is a normal fact of life, and indeed W.L. Phelps wrote, "The expression 'right as rain' must have been invented by an Englishman."

Missing Marie

Red chipped bowls
hand-me down clothes
a bright blue tea kettle
dented where I dropped it once
& never told her
Disorder in cupboards
where she defined order
shelf paper crimpling—
her smoothing
never took

I let all die
trudged like a blinder
through mines, months
just getting by
without the sun
A weed had its way
on the patio balcony
from which she approved
creek and forest view,
our slight shift upward

Blooming regularly
with no help from me
white and red flowers
like petite roses
penciling her walk
This spring
their colors
seemed too bright
insane or giddy
with her passing

She told me
she spent afternoons
dancing with Cancer
in her nodes and lungs
without tune
no witness
never wanting
to be a bother
praying God would grant her
a little more future

I work where doctors
save lives from Cancer
as easily as golfing nine
On TV they go
"Hey you! You are Cancer free!"
But not Marie
She was their anomaly
They put a death bell
inside her, a foreign
Chemistry

They weren't sure.
Is anyone ever?
Faith will show you
a person's absence
opens a space
evolving necessarily
the way a flock
of plain black birds
alighting tree to tree
makes room for the next

I focused on landing my daughter
where she would feel safe
Yet, in fading daylight,
I did not forget
Marie's last Friday afternoon
alive and grinning
in her hospital bed
at a rudderless ceiling
I am so happy
I have a grand daughter

My letting weeds
have their wistful way
"Oh Lord!" she'd say,
and trim the clutter
Now I have two
tentative plants
one with white-rimmed
waxy leaves
the other, a ruby-green
grocery store climber

Scarves

I would phone Sundays
from the park at the bottom of our hill
Not much of a park, I'd say, toggling litter and butts,
Still a park, you'd say
An eagle has mapped a triangular route over our apartment
Several days now, about noon, he takes over from the clouds
I wonder whether anyone else is looking up
A crane carves a wide swath over the K-Mart parking grid—
I've seen him two miles southwest, two northeast
dogged as a paintbrush: temporal and gaudy
I don't want to give up

I wear your scarves like lion tails
Everyone says I was so brave
waiting for the antique clock to chime each half hour
hovering near your hospital bed moored in the living room
me imagining you would soon wake and say something
Everyone fretted over whether we had the proper thermometer
but taking your temperature was a knee jerk reaction
to a listless immobility that could not be repaired
Skinny and frail
Water sinking back into the sockets
You'll be ok, I said,
I know, you said

Scarves are wisps of color, blind desperation
adding a vestige of grace or bravado
shielding a head from glare and rain
One day I am wearing a leopard print scarf on the South Street bus
A woman across from me twists nearly the same pattern
Wider spots
Kindred splotches, motherless
Lost on a bus that leads nowhere

One afternoon in sleepy fugue
a poem breathes from snow
each flake a cell
petitioning impetus
whitewashing white…
But I could never write anything down
It was always a rush to the bathroom

Who put on her pants?
Our helper scolded
The catheter cord streaming from the crotch
not neatly down the left leg
Our haphazard procedure
I'm sorry, I said,
And I'm sorry, too, you
bewildered, infantile
Who would recognize the lifetime Bridge-Master?
The sergeant who once taught radar to the Chinese?

I don't memorialize you when I wear the scarves
but feel a little better
catch my goofy face in a mirror
hear you chiming, what's not to like
The wind lifts just right over the eaves in a dry whistle
A clink in the kitchen like us making breakfast
Never can put a finger on anything
Remember we used to say *scruff*?

I've never been an indelible person
What if my brain splits open like a plum?
All the what ifs crowding my night-time, clotting stars?
Your shimmering reality crossing over
Your Fox News heroes: Megyn and Brett
echo all you didn't tell me

From half a piece of bacon to a nibble to none
From four, three, two raspberries to one
Finally, I pushed tiny pieces of orange Popsicle through the grate
Turning bones slightly every few minutes so you could breathe

But it didn't help me, it didn't help you
Days dripping wax into other days

Your Saudi throw: camels ornately attired atop our cat-scratched carpet
doesn't recall your utopian Republican bellow
Maybe I should drink more, look for a ghost
in inebriated glimpses of dawn or dusk
The lake was stoic, bone-cold when we visited
turning its back on me
A shadow pulling starlight
through your good eye

Now it is June
I fudge the temperature dial, jimmy our air conditioning
Always something isn't it, you'd say
Mesmerized as if by a thin paper-doll cutout of troubles holding hands
you saw people in the corners of the large room where you were marooned
a man and a boy
You thought we'd been in a car accident together
Don't worry they are coming for us

It snowed all night
No one wanted to come down the drive
Do we really need to? Our hospice nurse, querulous,
who pronounced you dead the moment she crossed the threshold?
Is that what they mean by the nick of time?
Didn't we get the last laugh?

Excerpts from *Writing Jimmy Carter's Autobiography*

I have so often been termed America's worst President
as well as a single hand clapping
to an unacknowledged demise of the Democratic Party,
that, in all honesty,
it's not part of my mirror anymore.
At one time I took it to bed with me, the word *failure*,
like a grape made sore and too soft,
rubbed again and again between soiled fingers.
I slept with it, wore its dark stain as a shield each morning,
ate it, swallowed, succored it, burped it—
a prized possession till it turned to stone.
I didn't throw it away, didn't want to lose its effect on me.

* * *

Growing up in the South, white or black,
taught one to grow a soul first, not second,
To make certain its vestments:
the eyes, the hands, were always steady.
Black children I saw
without shoes heading for run-down schools
did not wear suffering as a badge I might.
Pain was deep in them as tree roots.
We whites suffered parasitically—
small scars on an almost beautiful face.

Screams we on occasion heard,
blinding as twelve suns
You had to close your eyes
for fear of losing all sight.
At times I lost consciousness and waited
for the church's bell to toll
A fury in my heart buried deep became raw.
It bubbled close to my lips
forcing me to smile
too wide and clench my teeth.

As I was born, a private joy to my parents in Plains,
Georgia's governor swayed and expanded like a syrupy praline
soaked in applause and laughter
at the Ku Klux Klan's annual ball.

* * *

It was a secret.
I lay out my sweaters while naked…
It may have appeared as though
I always wore the same cardigan,
blue button-down,
a thin brown cross-stitch. In truth,
I had many sweaters, many
shades of blue, various mohair
and sailors' cable-stitch,
no two interchangeable.
Roz and I chuckled in private
about the anchorman's unchecked lust
for my quiet lust,
a self-contained chuckle
with my very best friend.
When I looked her in the eye,
it was enough.
Skirts fell away.
Our spirits rose to the arched ceiling
without argument.
But the sweaters were my secret and
thoughts I had while making a deft selection of style or color.
The poet may think of lime or lemon, if citrus
be what the sun needs
of shallow peelings,
grapes falling
to a rotting river's bottom, an old woman's teeth,
of ocean arc, whip and spray,
of all the hard things people must do
and the simplest pleasures:
slicing cold butter,
singing loudly over a parade.

* * *

I never learned to rush…
Growing up in the South
we didn't really have time for it.
I hear about the stress it causes:
Is it equivalent to the stress of sitting still,
looking dully into a day devoid of opportunity?

Amiri Baraka once said
Why should any man or woman run to be someplace at a certain time?
When he or she is capable of walking with dignity and grace to arrive
at the right time?

Do you think suddenly of helicopters?
Over dusky roofs maneuvering
with M42s poking out, silver noses…
The wrong time; the wrong means?
A failure of language, or simply drama?
Occasionally, Shakespeare
puts in principle
what would never make us laugh in practice.

* * *

I have studied nobility in weary faces of Native American chiefs.
Yet, the world over I note
people who crave peace without appeasement
cannot ascend the arc of nobility to attain it—
So much stands in the way: food, water, an open sky.

I wonder, was
Darkness not a dream God had
of shadow-less calm and repose
To breathe and walk in peace among friends, the dead
As well as the living?
For one does not imagine God sleeping ever…
Would that be the end of all things?
Two sides racing across a bridge
to the middle?

* * *

Joys of the South were
as resonant as difficulties
A spare cotton field after harvest
The aching wet barnyard smell, pepper pinpricks,
An ochre moon rising overhead, occasional night bird
How I loved Keats, and Dylan T.!

I can't say God wanted me to be President
(*President of what?* My mother asked…)

It was I who craved a gentleness without tears
who had ambition
my secret in the dark and in the light
before the mirror and the mirror inside…
Who I am
angles, stealth and pride.
By our good works, do we make ourselves
shiny?

* * *

We had to move home to Plains,
Family business
My father's passing
I became a peanut farmer for real then
Roz, officer's wife, small-town miserable,
steadied herself with bookkeeping, cooking for vagabonds,
befriending Negro neighbors
despite burning lawns, and makeshift Cross

Sometimes in the unnerving shadows of night,
questions of simple reality are ominous.
I check off a bad dream,
I flip through my misgivings
from an imperfect childhood,
I stick to my mother's fawning wishes as a fly
on flypaper.

Because I cannot answer daily family questions,
I undertake the larger public life,
where my actions ring steadfast, sonorous,
Pour real cement where a curb is needed.

* * *

American baseball is a leisurely sport.
Its strategies are endless, and the clock isn't ticking.
Its clichés never let me down.
One day my lover threw me a curve ball, walked out forever.
If you can't play ball with the big boys, get out of the park.

Marcel Duchamp understood time through chess,
that thinking, short or long, is the game itself
Not prediction, not happenstance—
Sweat on an opponent's brow,
Crack of wood on a hard fastball,
Stealthy advance, pawn by pawn,
The tease to steal
like courting
and later, marital sex,
a superb game with rules intrinsic to fairness
respecting the talents of each player…
Reminiscent of coming to the table at Camp David,
or being submerged for days under water waiting to surface behind an
enemy marker.

I stared absentmindedly at my croissant, as Anwar talked,
and thought about drifting snow, flake by flake, no pattern of relief
I thought about freedom and belief,
recalled Malraux saying
"Freedom is not an exchange—it is freedom."
No one ever wants to give in, yet the world is populated
by those who do and those who don't.

In Another League

My daughter cuts figure eights
at Merry Place Park,
cycling in and out of view.
Through a play fort's wooden planks,
her bobbing pink Barbie helmet—
never out of my sight
more than four seconds tops.
Cold wind on my face,
fingers in my thinning hair,
tears crisp lashes.
"There they are!"
She slides up breathless.

I look into a new blue space
not one hawk, but two
darting right before us, then
three smaller spirallers,
a whole family of majesty.
They come close, as if called,
perform flamboyant
groundswell dips,
churn up again,
the young ones sword-like mimics.
I have a camera in my hands
but the moment freezes.

They circle up over the trees
and kettle down.
My daughter leads me
deeper into the woods.
Craning necks toward their nest,
Don't you love to adventure? she says.
The path is thick with brambles, muddy
foreign pipes and sewage drains.
Not a sweet forest such as I dimly

recollect from childhood,
but the best refuge we find
outside the city.

The hawks reign here—
an aerie high unseen.
They've created a nest
from the impossible
barrage of litter and twigs,
where a creek snakes
a scar in the earth's
numb cheek.
Vehicles thunder past
on the highway behind us—
a collateral wind
waterfall of sound.

My sadness starched
with blues and greens
now ironed out,
a smile comes back.
My daughter and I proclaim
our private happiness,
blessed by a grace we cannot
touch nor taste…
loosely knit shells
over cobblestone light,
hawks fluttering in
and out of view.

Progress Montage

The law of progress holds that everything now must be better than what was there before. Don't you see if you want something better, and better, and better, you lose the good. The good is no longer even being measured. –Hannah Arendt 1974

I live in the city of the Walt Whitman Bridge, but I am not Walt Whitman
I have walked through its subway turnstiles forward and back
Given dollars to a homeless man selling newspapers and considered myself conciliatory
Worked diligently, paid my rent, queued mindfully for the streetcar, sorted recycle from garbage
I am a resilient bleary-eyed commuter, with a citizen's leverage
I have voted, cooked nutritious dinners, carefully buried my parents

I think about the foxglove purple of the woman's hair as she talks to herself
I look down at my shoes and I wonder whether today's check will clear
I fancy falling in love with a Septa bus driver
Soldiering on, perched next to him
Tearing this ruby-gray city open—the color of eggplant flesh
Taxis and streetlights the seeds inside

I feel like howling but I am not Allen Ginsberg
I am not Leonard Cohen vetting his soul in darkness against God
Nor David Bowie raising Lazarus for the last time
I have danced at underground arts union station trocadero electric factory purple-lit punk
Listened to benevolent home-grown and immigrant chatter, the garbled city sighing
Wanted a lot of things I could not have and accepted things I didn't ask for

Oh, heart, I say, call out as any heart dreams of calling
Not accounting for sensitivity of light or probability of battling
An imaginary stringed instrument inside one's body dying to be plucked
A rosebush held fast by its own thorns and bracken
Waiting to puncture the spring night air
I reach out my hands with his oak knots for knuckles

Walt walking through smoke, rubble, bandaging flesh that yet held soul
I don't cry anymore just feel sick inside when people
Make each other miserable
I want to believe as I used to believe
Words, leaves of a spacious tree,
The spine of the perfect oratory

Walt, the bridge is your beautiful green, a shimmering arc of wire steel
and light
Persuading us how you loved the sea, her rhythms the pulsating blood
Of every soldier you cradled, perishing in your arms
Our emotional tangential future
Brought forth in that generation
Walt Whitman, bare feet in the sand, writing another soliloquy

In the inky night tumbler, the sky's whorls and the wind's pining
What say you, how the voice holds its shudders, its thunder
Stretched thin across a dark field's midriff, a barn, a few horses
What we know we can walk toward
Say I love you I love you
If you cannot hear yourself think, if you cannot persist

CODA

In Kenya's Rift Valley, student Evie Clarke, age 14, sees Venus, Mars
and *loads of suns*
Poised on the equator, squinting through a travelling telescope,
She secures a version of herself as astronomer
In awe of seven new earth-sized planets
39 light years away, circling a dwarf star named Trappist-1

Walt transported ice cream through as many hospital wards as he could
trek in a day,
Though some of the men sure cannot live, mother,
They quite well enjoyed it
There is a silent place I have not yet earned where salt water roils perfume
Brave notations double-back and bloom
And a fire burns and burns

My Covid Swim

– after Bruce Cockburn's "Pacing the Cage"

I wanted to write a poem
Perfect as my Covid swim
The Atlantic Ocean grey and roiling
Me another swell within.
Brighter than its silvery welts
Surer than a tree
I'm diving in
Shivering, free.

I stretch and bob while floating
Lucky whale lolling near a reef
Our lives are so uncertain now
Salt lips bring relief.
I tell myself hold fast this moment.
Think of what's truest in your heart.
You can't cry in the ocean when it's this cold,
Still I'm falling apart.

Consider floaters from doomed ships
Lost to endless sway and sky.
When finally, they arrive
They don't pause for thankless whys.
If they'd never launched from land
They'd never been so lost,
Nor fully understand
The worth of the cost.

Words cannot touch
What I scrape within.
Reaching for the warm, fluttery life
While casting only its skin.
It's blue, really blue, and cold,
So cold, whitening you
To your core.
Nothing hurts anymore.

Prayer for George

i

After the ceremony
scotch, neat
my mother's best crystal
me unseemly pajamaed
white as bean paste
no privilege by proxy
ungodly hot my apartment
not on fire as the Reverend Al
not a burning neck pressed to cement
just hot enough to flick a switch
electric air,
not God's air for breath

ii

One's name—that's important—
Picasso's signature became art
Sharpton knows his is the name of an enslaver
Callous owner of his great-grandparents
He makes his voice art

iii

At the university community town hall
the black medical student is asked to represent
You're from Colorado? Oh really?
That's where it starts.
White people ask what it feels like to be me...
Why don't they already know this?
Telling you these stories
doesn't make me feel better.

iv

George let his niece scratch his head after work
He played hoops, liked a laugh
Religious mentor
to Third Ward youth
Human guy, regular
reducible to breath to body
His family in front of the cameras,
His sister his voice in the courtroom
Fighting for justice, praying
That fear would exhaust itself
That we might change

Coltrane and David at Work

–David B. Roth, MD, PhD, is the Simon Flexner Professor and Chair of Pathology and Laboratory Medicine, University of Pennsylvania Perelman School of Medicine

Make a list—set goals—go outside—come back in.
Stretch on yoga mat. Make soup.
Watch no news whatsoever.
Let your head fall to pillow, a droplet on a map.
Watch daily news briefings—
graphed deaths like crooked arthritic fingers.

My apartment is so small
but with John Coltrane here
it feels immense
joyful notes mortared to sorrow
leaning back into my chair, eyes closed
walls fall away
I'm not much tied to incidentals,
but as his tenor sax snakes
through a miniature brass camel caravan
my parents bought decades ago in Egypt
coiling around the cleft hooves of the baby with barely one hump
I see themes of a new world, one not unkind to me
but equally unimpressed
with everything human, even the bruised yellow flowers
in a geometrically absurd clay vase I brought from the desert
when I thought of home as a warm merry den—
staging area for daily intercourse, commerce, my life
that doesn't exist here today
now that Coltrane has pushed out the walls,
and time's unmetered storms are imminent
one might venture graciously a question
even advocate
What can I do today?
Shadows float familiar memories
as clocks tick, John's horn spikes, and a pianist takes the challenge to heart
Today?

Tear up your list. Call a friend.

Confession

You were the one to remind me
what a mess I'd been, my hair matted,
my eyes dull as stone.

You were the one who said
I shouldn't be alone.
We were bonded.

Every night I held the blue pill
under my tongue till the nurse disappeared,
then crept to your room where you took it.

You couldn't sleep and I didn't want to.
Enough to build a marriage, we thought,
our meal trays hooked together.

You wrote letters to your father
asking forgiveness. Would he?
Sure, I said. But no letters came.

The whole thing was awful. Still,
Shirley, our schizophrenic race car driver,
kept us in cigarettes, and we laughed

the day a priest came to exorcize my roommate.
"They're ousting the devil from his rightful home
behind the sink!" But who would believe us,

till the shrieking began? We were hopeful
the day you packed. I gave you all the money I had,
but it was only money and not enough.

You're the nicest, I said, the nicest of all.
You are, you said, and squeezed me tight. Even now,
I don't know what we were trying to do.

You called once, later; you'd checked out
again, only to find yourself
alone in another hospital. Would I call?

Would I? I must have walked through rooms for years,
looking past places we would have put things:
our blue parrot, drawings I'd made of our friends.

The World Series

It was the fourth game of the World Series
and I believe it was raining.
We were all gathered in a room.
Each had a team, a cheese sandwich, a beer.
I had never really understood the World Series
(& it scared me to think how many
watch that game, together, alone, wherever)
but I was watching so closely that night
that when it rained harder, I heard sobbing
and the voices inside the men saying "get up, get up"
when the second baseman slipped in the mud.
Somebody hit a home run and our hearts leapt
into that damn ball—we went flying right out
of the park. It was that kind of a game.
Suddenly I knew but I couldn't get the words
out of my mouth fast enough
out into the world
where one night a man will tell you
he used to be a blue bird.
But tonight, maybe it's late, or you're tired, or things
make sense all at once
and not at all…
when he says it again,
blue bird,
believe him.

In this world some ask
why does Snow White wear red shoes?
Why is the apple red…the sun…the blood?
And some carry the question against their hearts
like a thorn. Some repeat it
repeat it till they are drunk.
Some say it's the apple.
A few eat the apple.
But tonight, all I can say is

I saw the World Series again
and I remember that last year
someone who lived once, died
someone who died a red death, lives
over and over, it could drive you crazy
except the World Series saved me once.
It was the only real thing in the room.
And I pushed finally
the words out of my
small voice, I said,
"Does anyone know why it's raining?"

Weightless

I can't explain it.
Your small hands pat
my back each fall
like soft pink orchids
ripe for one more moon.
Those nights I was sick
you corralled angels
from the bent shadows of trees
to lead me back—
sweet sighs, like grace.
One midnight you
struggled closer
to nuzzle my body
against my fear.
We were each stunned
by the grief of the other.

I had to love you twice:
once for myself,
once for our father,
who could not speak of you
without soaring to the ceiling—
a monster of welts and punches.
When he read the story aloud,
the dark hall of his voice
convinced me it was you
lost forever
in the emerald land of Oz,
you who might return
when the witch's laugh
was menacing, you who could do
what we could not.

You were my brother,
inalterably small, but
strangely wry, with plans
all your own.
Lonely bell-tolled hours
in quiet bars
I find myself thickening
like dust on scuffed hardwood floors
as knots appear in a stranger's face.
Reaching through the eyes
with my crooked heart,
I promise, Brother,
you'll never play Hansel again.

We swindled the wizard,
stormed the drawbridge,
escaped unharmed together,
me carting you along—
tiny living corpse—
padlock and key.
I am scared, Brother,
to let you go on
weightless in another life…

Bag of Wind

Never set sail
without your bag of wind.
This the mariners knew
by heart. From
nonbelievers
they strode apart.
Each year's end
bustling cargoes
silk and honey, spices
and rope coiled tight—
death drums—
appeared as
they jibed: did I, Dear?
Did you?
Disappear?

Old women of the Shetlands
and the Hebrides
still sell their bags of wind,
stolen wares from a napping god,
rising up from the bluestone
and the round water chapel.
The old ladies lean out along the pier,
waving their bags of wind
for three tuppence or less,
when all have sworn forth,
'cept a few drifters who steer
downwind along the shore,
calling, did I, Dear?
Did you?
Disappear?

Never set sail, love,
without your bag of wind
for nights are unkind—

a storm in front, a squall behind—
when you can't let go
of the trembling
in your mind…
that there's nothing to find
in the tumbling or the fury
of the sea, the sky, the sun
and the queer blue slumber
whose lapping dreams you fear…
Did I? Did you?
Did I, Dear?
Disappear?

The Robin of the System

—for my daughter, Maya, and in memory of David Foster Wallace

Coldest morning in twenty years
commuters shuffling, rubbing limbs,
cursing the train again for being late
coaxing bitter warmth from chuckles
Main Line cancelled...AHA HA!
Squinting into the sun,
I tighten my wool scarf over my nose, mouth and ears.
Across railway tracks:
a stoic assembly of robins
ornaments a skeleton of tree branches.
Their orange chests puff like water balloons.
Tiny spouts of white air spiff from their engines.
Two scouts fly off to distant haunts.
The resilient lift their beaks
sip what sunlight pauses.
Tough nuts: no gibbering.
They don't huddle into each other, yet
one can tell they have a system.
The scouts return, the band advances:
a shock of even colder air hits us all below.
It isn't the first time I wish I were a bird.
It won't be the last.

As any mom,
I want to be the best mom.
Friends warn me:
what we remember is not what a child remembers.
Be brave, I say, be happy
but fear curls beside us with its cold clock hands.
You want to be the best child.
But you don't know what is possible.
Now we queue adult to adult,
like a shimmering mirror.

Caught in a snow globe,
I abandon my car one evening.
I can't get up any hill
and even slipping down is treacherous.
I triage with two Comcast guys,
waiting for them to maneuver
their jack-knifed vans.
They can't help me, they say,
I could sue their company.
It's an easier journey on foot.
The hushed world now pinked along its edges,
only the creek is gurgling
as I wend a path through the woods.
A crazy whoosh startles me from behind.
An avalanche of shape and form,
four deer clatter through snowy brush.
They eye me for a moment.
So what no feather beds!
No slaves to metal either—
no steering inside it,
no fingering it in a pocket.

I am not a skeptical or cynical person.
I've loved the world outright: cobbled roads, milky stars,
our daily industry edged by shadow.
I've been a fool, but each moment has been worth its surprises.
I knew a man, a genius, who was wounded by the beautiful.
He knew we humans don't have a system.
He let go.

It's a predictable move
to idealize the natural lives of animals—
how they hang on. They are fierce that way.
As your mom, I say, hang on.
The time you take is your time.
As a fellow voyager, I trust
clear, sweet air after a storm,
sun searing snow into diamonds,
and, later, dappling the driven water.

Thanksgiving

—for my sister Leslie

i
50 feet of yard way back
Our "Paradise"
Sunflowers and pollywogs
Limestone and mulch

I loved getting my hands dirty
The feel of hot rocks on my feet
Sandy cemeteries with spirit wisps
That I was left to roam free

I owe my parents everything
Arc of fern, its cucumber smell,
Fluttering green lace
See-through as a mayfly wing

I owe them my love of water
Droplets, snowflakes, shore rings, fog
The way a river winds out of sight
And you follow on with your eyes

ii
Our parents crashed into things
Too big molecules in the rascal brew
Yes, it was hard to follow
But instructive if you braved it

I cursed them through my twenties
As we threw martinis down
A love hate tussle
Like a bad pop song

How we all squeezed through
The storm's eye into a future

Not remarkable but peaceable enough
As their winter's passing

I could do some hereditary digging
Tap-tap spade our lineage
Muck and tarred chromosomes
What quality does my daughter take across the ice?

iii
Floating on my back in the waters
I face the sky
An eagle crosses my vision
A loon calls to another loon

Children at camp across the way
Scream splash giggle
I close my eyes tight
Tiger eyes around the sun

We've sold their lake home,
Their slice of heaven
How does the other half live?
I hear dad say

In some public place
Where I least expect
I will burst into tears
And disappear

Fireflies

–for Julie Willson

We were once
the makers of stars
and now we must invent ways
to get them back.
We string fireflies together
by their spindly ashen legs
to fly up brightly, to retrieve
the stars. It doesn't matter
what we never have…the fireflies'
silent singing upward,
isn't that enough?
Remember the night
we were so beautiful we couldn't stand it,
dancing, spinning, people around us
chanting, "Faster!"
We could die now
because we have seen enough.
But travelling on, we take all
the curses with us. We, the makers
of stars, always unlacing
our dreams. Crystal quiet now,
Death in transit, we could make
the stars ice, could make them melt,
then catch them with our tongues,
to swallow everything whole, fresh, pure
Dessert. Like strawberries
our stars. Like peaches.
But listen,
everyone wants us to be blind
and give up. & that as we go on
blind, giving up darkness, giving up

surety, giving up our pinings, the way,
the way of life. I love
our destiny of trying not
to reclaim what has always been ours
but of loving this world
as it has never been
but ached for.

Indefinitely

How long we live, maybe
A little longer
With a definitive linkage: breath to breath

No bridge we can easy over
To picnic the other side...cucumbers, dill, raspberries, cream
Ground warm toes
Nothing lifeless above, below

We could build a bridge precise texture of weighted materials
Placing bricks as we expressed them where exposed was air
Or say...just surveying the property, not claiming
Space, the moon's terror, responsibility
Of stars
Giddy light, our laughter

ii
Someone wanted to believe in it
Indefinitely
I sat in the holy coffee shop, heard a poet groan
The relationship is over

Indefinitely...suspicious life sentence, frantic to jump ship without a buoy
At very short notice

Indefinitely time it is, not the time it is
Not
No commitment to either state of being,
No commitment to sky to water

Are the pea pods fresh, do you sell false beams?
(to resuscitate the hardware man, the grocer)
Not really, not exactly

iii

Don't nod your head and say
You're right, probably,
Don't stop listening

Stubbed toe, dark trough throat
On and on, not admitting truth beside the falsity of things
That beg to be thrown away but cannot be thrown

As in love, indefinitely, equals
Theoretically, no reason to fly

Leaving Edinburgh on the Evening Train

We observe each other in the glass
the dark-eyed Pakistani girl,
her brother and myself,
until I am able to look
through them and match their foreheads,
wrinkling with a question, to the waves
of the bright North Sea.
The finest sprays,
spreading like fingers
in their black hair, make me
put my hand to the glass
to feel the tactile image of the cold
which must inhabit the heart
when one refuses comfort.
When the parents begin to shift
to look askance at me and whisper,
the boy startles me with English,
"My mother tells us to go to sleep,"
and the girl nods.
The North Sea is getting darker
and darker without sun
and what little light
is left in me
seems also to go out.
Night begins to draw the outline, erasing
all color of the girl
watching over her brother.
His head thumps lightly
on the glass
like someone forever knocking.

When we arrive, everyone smiles,
gathering their things as though
nothing has happened.
I step freely into the station
up and up the escalator until
only three steps left, I turn
for the last look as if
I were really parting.
In the throng below, the face
of the Pakistani girl
is the only face I see, lost,
searching. But her family
is just yards away
calling her to the next platform.
Moving towards them, she looks up
and in that instant
as she finds me and smiles
I believe I am forgiven
for not saying goodbye.

About the Author

Luellen Fletcher enjoyed being part of the undergraduate writers' workshop at the University of Iowa, and graduated Phi Beta Kappa in 1979 with a BA in English. A Sloan Scholarship recipient, she studied Modern British Poetry at Lincoln College, Oxford University, and completed an MFA in creative writing in 1986 from the University of Arizona in Tucson. She and poet-colleague Will Jennings coordinated Potlatch, a free city-wide arts festival in Iowa City, spring 1978, taking inspiration from the Oregon Country Fair. Fletcher was part of the Tucson Poetry Festival Committee for four years, and Festival Co-Director in 1994. She also helped incorporate poetry and small press events into the Rocky Mountain Book Festival, collaborating with writers from Denver's coffeehouse circuit.

Fletcher has worked at the University of Pennsylvania in the Department of Pathology and Laboratory Medicine since 1999, currently serving as Associate Director for the Path BioResource, a consortium of shared resources that provide biomedical technology and expertise to researchers. She chairs Penn and Pencil Club, sponsored by Penn's Kelly Writers House for faculty and staff writers. Before moving to Philadelphia, she taught composition and literature to community college students. She currently volunteers as a writing tutor for college students through JEVS Human Services.

CPSIA information can be obtained
at www.ICGtesting.com
Printed in the USA
LVHW031057060821
693983LV00001B/5

9 781664 164987